The Im

How Winners Turn Practice into Success

By Mike Tully

Copyright 2012 1st Edition, Mike Tully
ISBN 978-1469993348 Published by TotalGamePlan, Inc.
900 Valley Road D-1, Clifton, NJ, 07013
Publishing date: March 2012

Disclaimer -- Any improper or missing credits for the stories and quotes contained in this book were unintentional. The author deeply regrets any errors or omissions.

DEDICATION

To my wife, Patty, who for years has practiced patience
with me and who is world-class at love and kindness.

TABLE OF CONTENTS

INTRODUCTION

By Carl McGown, Ph.D.

A few years ago, I was invited to speak at an exclusive private high school. The topic was "What It Takes to Become Great."

I thought the speech was really very good, but the audience didn't seem to share my enthusiasm. Perhaps this statement is what got me in trouble: Talent doesn't exist.

The parents at this school didn't want to hear that. They had grown up in a world where their own talents were considered innate, and they wanted to think that their children were also blessed with inherent talents like intelligence, musical ability or athletic prowess.

That's not the way things work. If there is such a thing as a talent gene, no one has been able to find it. Just the opposite is happening. The deeper scientists dig, the more they find that skill comes from something called deliberate practice.

I've seen the result of correct practice in years of coaching volleyball at the college and international levels. I've seen unrecruited players become all-Americans. I've seen unlikely candidates become Olympic team stars.

That was their reward for putting in the hours, and for practicing the right way. Those athletes did a better job of improving than the people around them.

Mike Tully is inviting you to do the same thing in "The Improvement Factor." He wants you to know how the best performers in the world got that way.

I met Mike years ago at a clinic for volleyball coaches. He always had a lot of questions. Still does. That curiosity has led Mike to explore the best ways to approach practice, and how to get rid of things that get in the way of improvement.

This book goes well beyond the sport arena, to areas like school and business. It's a roadmap for, well, greatness.

I still think the people at that school got very good advice.

CHAPTER ONE

Your Game Has Just Begun

"Every artist was first an amateur." -- **RALPH WALDO EMERSON**

One day Hall of Fame baseball player Ted Williams watched a teammate return to the dugout after striking out.

"Tell me," Williams said. "When you swung and missed that ball, did your bat go over the ball or under it?"

"What difference does it make," the teammate wanted to know. "Either way, I struck out."

It makes all the difference in the world, Williams explained. Knowing how you missed was the first step in preparing for the next time.

This kind of thinking was central to Williams' greatness. He always wanted to improve. Events were never as important as what he could learn from them. For his teammate, a strikeout meant that the game was over. For Williams, it meant the game had just begun.

This book is about whether your game is over or just begun. If you believe the game has just begun, this book is valuable. If you think the game is over, this book is essential.

It will tell you about the world's great performers, and how they turn practice into success.

Their habits can become your habits. Their thoughts can become your thoughts. Their journey to success can become yours.

On my journey, I've met people who have helped me see that life is about skill, not talent. Renowned sports psychologist Dr. Rob Gilbert, world-class volleyball coach Dr. Carl McGown and team-builder extraordinaire Gary Pritchard all inspired me to look into what makes people great at what they do.

"You have everything you need already inside you," Dr. Gilbert tells those who believe they don't have what it takes.

"Initial ability and final ability are not closely related," adds Dr. McGown, emphasizing that you can become as skilled as you make up your mind to be.

Fred McMane, a dear friend and mentor whom I met during my sports writing days, used our company softball team to make a point about life. "People work like they play," he said. "I can tell you how someone will behave in the office just by watching them play softball."

Fred's point was that attitudes and work habits translate from one area of life to another. His wisdom will be alive in this book. Even though I'll be using lots of examples from the world of sports, the information can help you improve anywhere: office, school, team, even in health and personal relationships.

Coach Pritchard introduced me to a quote attributed first to novelist Robert Louis Stevenson and then to writer and radio commentator Richard L. Evans. "Never be discouraged. Everyone who got where they are had to begin where they were."

If you're looking for specific advice on how to hit a tennis ball or on how to play the guitar, you won't find it here. Someone else can help you with that. Here you'll find ideas that will make your tennis or guitar practice more productive.

Never be discouraged. I don't know where you are now, but by using the principles in this book, you won't be there for long.

CHAPTER TWO

The Most Important Skill

"There's always room for improvement. It's the biggest room in the house." -- **LOUISE HEATH LEBER**

During the 2004 football season, Tom Coughlin felt his coaching career slipping away. Despite his success at Boston College and then for the NFL Jacksonville Jaguars, Coughlin was in trouble and he knew it.

His fierce style was keeping him from connecting with players. The wins were too infrequent, and New York Giants fans were chanting, "Fire Coughlin!" If he couldn't get his players to absorb his words -- his game plans, strategy, counsel -- he would lose his team for good and then, for sure, his job.

That's when Coughlin turned to one of his most trusted players, Kurt Warner, and asked for a favor.

"Go home and make a list of all the things you think I need to do better as a coach," Warner recalled Coughlin saying. "And don't hold back."

Warner did just as Coughlin requested, returning with pages of feedback. Coughlin read it all and used it. A 58-year-old man with a history of accomplishment within his industry did not ignore the need to continue to learn, adapt and improve. Coughlin wasn't fired. Instead, he has won two Super Bowls and might wind up in the Hall of Fame because of his willingness to keep an open mind.

*** *** *** *** ***

Let's face it: No matter what you're doing, someone wants you to do it better. If you're in sales, your boss wants more closings. If you're drafted by a sports team, the coach wants you to raise your game. Baseball umpires like to say, "We're the only profession where you have to be perfect on the first day and get better after that."

They're only half right. They're correct about the need to perfect their craft. They're wrong if they think they're the only ones who must meet this high standard. What would you think of an airline pilot, a surgeon or a dentist who was less than perfect when it came to serving you?

Sad to say, hardly anyone gives improvement the credit it deserves. People tend to take two views of it. First there's the "Beautiful Sunset" reaction, in which we marvel at someone who has improved, much the way we look at a beautiful sunset. Wow, we say. Look at that! But just as we don't ponder the spectrum of colors and the scattering of light at sundown, we don't think about what actually goes into improving.

Then there's the "Walk and Chew Gum" view, which we see a lot at athletic banquets. That's when coaches give out awards to the Most Improved Player. Too often it's a throwaway gift to someone who works hard and has a good attitude. The unspoken text is: "At the start of the season, he/she couldn't walk and chew gum at the same time. Now he/she can."

Both the Beautiful Sunset and the "Walk and Chew Gum" views are wildly incorrect. Improvement isn't something that just happens. It comes from really, really hard work: conscious effort, well-designed practice, thousands of repetitions and tons of feedback. That's why Coughlin and people who win the Most Improved Player Award are the ones to watch in our society.

So says Dr. Anders Ericsson, known as the "expert on experts" for his study of how people get good at what they do. He writes that by viewing top performers not simply as experts in their own field "but as experts in maintaining high levels of practice and improving performance, we are likely to uncover valuable information ..."

In other words, people who have learned how to improve at one thing deserve our complete attention, because they may well have learned the secret to improving at anything.

Remember Dr. Ericsson's words if you come upon a bottle on the beach, and a genie pops out and says you can have any skill you wish. Ask for the ability to improve. It's the most important skill of all, because it can help you get better at everything you do.

*** *** *** *** ***

U.S. President Barack Obama, for one, would love it if you became world-class at improvement. In a 2011 jobs address, he told Americans, "If we want (companies) to start here and stay here and hire here, we have to be able to out-build and out-educate and out-innovate every other country on Earth."

In other words, we've all got to find a way to get better.

Americans need improvement more than ever. Think of it. As in no other era, people must create their own future. Traditional jobs have gone away, perhaps never to return.

Millions of people are changing careers. Baby Boomers are trying to learn computer skills that 10-year-olds take for granted.

There's only one problem with all this need to get better. Most people don't know how to do it. They practice, but they get less from their sweat and precious practice time than they could.

This book changes everything for student-athletes, career-switchers, coaches, teachers, employers. It offers one theme: No matter who you are, you can improve at what you love and need.

And I'm not talking about improvement that gets your school average from a "C" to a "B+." I'm talking about dramatic improvement, the kind that can astonish you and those around you, place you at the top of your field and give you success, stature and satisfaction you never dreamed would belong to you.

This kind of improvement has nothing to do with innate ability. It has to do with learning how the great performers go about their business, and modeling their actions, attitudes and habits.

In this book, there are nine strategies for world-class improvement. Any one of them will help you get better at what you do. You can use these strategies in any order or combination. There's just one exception. You've got to do the first one, "Eat an Orange Every Day." Without that one, you'll never reach the greatness that lies within your grasp. So let's get going.

CHAPTER THREE

Eat an Orange Every Day

"I hate housework! You make the beds, you do the dishes and six months later you have to start all over again." -- **JOAN RIVERS**

John Vill'Neuve was trying to put a man on the moon. This was back in the 1960s, when the race in space was just as much about beating the Russians as it was about exploration.

Vill'Neuve was in the race. He was project manager for the team that was building the navigation system for the lunar lander. That, plus a wife, six kids and a mortgage, meant a lot of pressure. He had a heart attack.

As part of Vill'Neuve's rehab, doctors told him to eat an orange every day. He listened and followed the instructions. For the rest of his life, he ate an orange every morning at breakfast.

It's the first strategy of world-class improvement, the same one that Tom Coughlin used: Identify what must be done, and make sure it gets done. Every day.

*** *** *** *** ***

For at least four days in his life, Tom Fleming was the best in the world at what he did. He won the New York City Marathon in 1973, setting a course record. Two years later, he did the same thing. He also won the Cleveland Marathon in 1978 and the Los Angeles Marathon in 1981. Later he went into teaching and coaching, where to this day he tries to pass along one message.

"Here's what parents and athletes have to realize," Fleming says. "To be really good, you have to do it every day."

*** *** *** *** ***

"Living Your Life Out Loud" by Salli Rasberry and Padi Selwyn tells the story of Mr. Amateau, who lived well past 100 years of age. Marveling at his health, the doctor asked Amateau the secret of his long life.

"I walk five miles every day," Mr. Amateau said.

"Five miles? Every day?"

"Every day," Mr. Amateau said.

"What do you do when it rains," the doctor pressed.

"I wear a raincoat."

*** *** *** *** ***

It turns out there was a simple genius to Vill'Neuve, Fleming and Mr. Amateau. They found the power that comes from doing something every day. They never let rain -- or anything else -- keep them from their necessary task. Their actions added up.

They lived by a principle expressed by inventor H. Joseph Gerber. "Rain puts a hole in stone because of its constancy, not its force." You'll see the same principle in the winds that carve the shapes in the rocks. Slow but sure effect.

As simple as this principle sounds, most people don't follow it. Instead, they multi-task. They procrastinate. They practice things they already know, rather than confront what they don't do well. Like a poor college student, they major in minor things.

Champions see a higher end, and build routines to match their vision. They don't spend life trying to fit in what's necessary; they build their lives around what is necessary.

Tennis legend Martina Navratilova came to a crossroads in her career, where she could have been just a good player or an all-time great. She chose greatness and the quest began with what she ate.

"When I started figuring it out, I wanted to figure it out all the way," Navratilova said in an article published in USA Today. "You can't just try to hit a great tennis shot. You need to get to the ball so you can hit a great tennis shot. So that means training. And if you really want to train hard, you need to fuel your body. So that means eating well. It's all-encompassing."

Navratilova developed a chain of success that went like this:

* Eat healthy.
* Healthy food feeds the body.
* A healthy body lets you train harder and better.
* Better training leads to better shots.
* Better shots lead to tournament victories.

Vill'Neuve had his own chain:

* Eat an orange every day.
* You regain your health.
* You get back to work.

15

* You help build the navigation system for the lunar lander.
* When astronaut Neil Armstrong needs the system, it's there and it works.

These chains are more than feel-good stories. They explain why some people achieve more than others. They can belong to you. One simple action, performed every day, can lead to miracles. Francis of Assisi said, "First do what is necessary, and then what is possible. Soon you will be doing the impossible."

Captain Sully Sullenberger paid tribute to the idea of daily practice after safely landing a jet in the Hudson River in 2009. His plane had lost power and in one instant he had to weigh his landing options. He chose to put the aircraft down in the river. He saved more than 100 lives. Later he said, "For the last 30 years I've been making small deposits every day. Today I made a large withdrawal."

Whether you're trying to fly a jet or win at tennis, you must do what these winners have done. You must find what you must do, then make sure you do it.

*** *** *** *** ***

So what exactly is your equivalent of living to be 100 like Mr. Amateau, or of winning the New York City Marathon or of putting a man on the moon?

What awe-inspiring achievement would you like to be yours? In what area would you like to acquire great skill and gain great advantage over your competition? For what endeavor would you be willing to invest hours and hours of practice? Take a look at your field, whether it's sales, sports, education or whatever. What exactly would you like? Do you want to be a pioneer? A recognized expert? Or simply the richest? Be as specific as possible when setting your target.

Once you know what you want to achieve, ask yourself what you must do to make this happen. What would be the one, single thing that could change your life? What is the one thing that, if you committed to doing it, would make a great difference in your preparation and results? In other words, what is your version of Vill'Neuve's orange?

There's just one problem with picking your orange. There are so many choices in life. This became vividly clear at a coaching clinic I attended one year in Iowa. The speaker was celebrated basketball coach Don Meyer, and his topic was "What I Wish I Knew Then."

Meyer, who coached 923 college victories, gave several tips to the coaches. He then referred them to his Web site, where they could find dozens more helpful hints. At a certain point, it was no use trying to take notes on Meyer's suggestions. There were too many!

Coach Meyer is just ONE source of information for any basketball coach wanting to get better. There are books, videos, lectures, conversations, movies, opinions, etc.

Plus, Meyers and basketball aside, every day is full of choices, beginning with the instant you wake up. Do you get out of bed or stay there for a while? Should you eat breakfast or skip it? If you're eating breakfast, do you sit down or eat on the run? And, by the way, what exactly should you eat?

Every day is filled with decisions. Amid all this information and opportunity, where do you begin to select an orange that will fit you perfectly? How does your brain synthesize all the input and produce a coherent strategy?

These are questions that will take lots of thought, and require trial and error. What works for others may not work for you. But you've got to search for something that you will do every day.

Your ideal orange would be:

* A simple, carefully selected action.
* That anyone can do.
* Performed daily.
* That will ripple into other areas of your life.
* And change your actions.

<u>Simple, Carefully Selected Action</u>

Whether they know it or not, great performers have an orange, something they do without fail. Some people, following doctors' orders, walk 10,000 steps a day. Or drink eight glasses of water. Outstanding school principals stand at the door every day and greet the students by name. Comedian Jerry Seinfeld made a practice of writing jokes every day. Nothing complicated about any of that.

"Almost all quality improvement comes via simplification," says business author and speaker Tom Peters.

"Simplicity is the ultimate sophistication," said Da Vinci.

Coach Mike Krzyzewski found a simple, perfect orange when he gathered the 2008 U.S. Olympic basketball players. As told in his book "The Gold Standard: Building a World Class Team," he challenged team leaders to come up with some shared values, something that could bring them together. The first thing they mentioned was being on time. Imagine that. Millionaire players with agents, personal Web sites and worldwide fame. Yet the first value they chose was something as simple as being on time.

There was wisdom to this choice. Being on time can reflect attention to detail, respect for the time of others, self-discipline, commitment to the team and equality among team members.

Here are some suggestions for a simple daily orange: eating a proper breakfast, adding nutritious foods, cutting out certain foods, writing your daily to-do list, taking the time to review practice, walking or running a certain distance or amount of time, keeping a journal, pausing to breathe or meditate, doing something out of your comfort zone, or doing a good deed for someone else.

That Anyone Can Do

The act should be so simple that anyone can do it. No need to run a marathon or solve complex equations. Just the opposite. The simpler the activity, the more likely you are to repeat it.

Years ago, I coached a wonderful athlete named Vanessa. One day at a team meeting, we challenged everyone to do something in world-class fashion. Vanessa said she would clean her cat's litter box as well as anyone could. Later that season, using that same dedication to all her tasks, she helped our team win a state championship. Vanessa took a simple but necessary task and did it in world-class fashion, just by deciding to do so.

Some people won't sustain even the simplest of tasks. For instance, could you make one phone call a day if it meant earning an easy $100? Years ago, motivational speaker Ed Agresta made an offer to a sports psychology class. He told the students that if they called his daily motivational hotline every day for 30 days, he would give them $100. All they had to do was dial, listen and leave a message to the effect of "I called today." Not one person did it.

So the vast majority of people are not willing to do something every day, even if the task is simple and there is a clear benefit. Imagine the edge you could gain on these people if you made the commitment and kept it!

Performed Daily

Your life is all about two words: CAN and WILL. You CAN eat an orange. But WILL you? Dr. Rob Gilbert demonstrated CAN and WILL in his sports psychology class at Montclair State University. He asked everyone if they could sing. Not opera or anything fancy. Just singing along to the radio in the car. Everyone agreed, yes, I can sing. Then Dr. Gilbert asked if anyone would volunteer to sing in front of the class. Only one person did. It was proof that everyone CAN, but not everyone WILL.

Here's a brief experiment to show where improvement begins. Think of something you don't feel like doing. Doing the dishes. Walking on a rainy day. Eating vegetables.

Once you've picked something you don't feel like doing, ask yourself this question: COULD you do it? The answer is, of course, yes. You COULD do it, whether you feel like it or not.

See? Daily attention to improvement is not a question of whether you CAN. It's a question of whether you WILL.

John Vill'Neuve ate his orange first thing in the morning. There was no such thing as putting it off until night came. Mr. Amateau walked no matter what the weather. Could you do what they did? Of course!

<u>That Will Ripple into Other Areas of Your Life</u>

The minute you select and perform your daily action, you may notice positive changes in other areas of your life. Jack McKeon, who once took the job of managing baseball's Florida Marlins -- at age 80 -- wrote a book called "Jack of All Trades." In it he urged people to get out of bed. That's it. Nothing more. Just get out of bed. Don't linger. Get up, start your day and do things! McKeon's chain could look like this:

* Get up earlier.
* You now have more time.
* You can use that time to work, exercise or eat a proper breakfast.
* You will be healthier and better prepared for your day.
* This will lead to increased success.

Oranges are everywhere among winners. There's a football coach in Florida who gathers his players before sending them home after practice. In a circle, they say "Return with honor," reminding each other to represent themselves well on and off the field. That's their orange, and you can bet that there have been times when this simple huddle changed the way some players behaved on their way to and from school. It rippled into other areas of their lives.

Dr. Ann Rasmussen, a family psychologist in Northern New Jersey, offers a simple action that immediately ripples into other areas of your life. She recommends pausing to breathe -- consciously -- five times a day. Inhale through the nose, exhale through the mouth, five times. And do this five times per day. The effect will astound you.

"This exercise will show you how you're idling," says Dr. Rasmussen, using the analogy of a car engine. Once you realize there is a more peaceful way to go through life, you can approach your tasks with less anxiety and stress.

A study published in 2011 indicated that people who kiss their spouse goodbye in the morning tend to make more money than people who don't. Why? Perhaps it's because the kissers take care with important details. Perhaps they tend to be more connected to what they do. Whatever the reason, there are causes and effects everywhere in life. For real improvement, do more of the things that produce good effects, and less of the things that yield bad ones.

And Change Your Actions

If you want more improvement and more success, you must change something in your life. To achieve change, you must undergo change. You must recognize situations and places where you know you will not attend to your tasks. You may even have to stop socializing with people who don't share your vision for a better future. Fashion publicist Kelly Cutrone says, "Stop sharing your dreams with people who try to hold you back, even if they're your parents."

For world-class improvement, your orange must change your life in some fundamental way. It must either remove something that's hurting you, or add something that will help you. Think of this statement: "One thing can change everything." And then look at this chain that comes from eating an orange every day:

* Oranges are really good for you.
* To eat an orange, you must have one available.
* To have one available, you must get one.
* To get oranges, you go to the produce section.
* In the produce section, there are other healthy foods.
* Surrounded by healthy foods, you may buy some.
* Once you buy them, you might eat them.

* The more you eat them, the healthier you become.

Imagine all that coming from one orange! This list does not even reflect the weight loss that will likely result, or the increased confidence that will come from the increased control you will exert over your life. This is what happened in Vill'Neuve's life. He (or someone in the family) spent more time in the produce section. They thought about oranges, never wanting to miss a day. Their thoughts and actions changed. That's what your orange should do: change your thoughts, actions and habits.

Here's an orange used by one of the top high school basketball coaches in the country. Bobby Hurley, leader of the nationally known program at St. Anthony's in Jersey City, N.J., says he makes it a point to compliment each player in the first 20 minutes of practice. It sounds simple, but Hurley must work hard to do this well. He must watch his players closely, looking for the good in them. Then he must actually give the compliments, not being distracted by the other things that go on in the gym every day.

*** *** *** *** ***

When faced with any commitment -- like a diet or a New Year's Resolution -- most people make a mistake. They see it as a test of their willpower. It's best to remember what actress Mae West said about willpower: "I generally avoid temptation unless I can't resist it."

Don't make your daily orange about willpower; make it about strategy. As long as you have the right strategy you can win. Vill'Neuve made sure to eat an orange as part of his breakfast. He put it into the rhythm of his life. There were no mistakes, never a day when he forgot. And the chain went forward to the moon.

Wade Boggs, a Hall of Fame baseball player, built several rituals and habits into his life, all designed to prepare him mentally and physically. He ate chicken before every game, and moved through his pregame routine on a minute-by-minute schedule. He ate, left his home and took batting practice on the precise minute.

John Ciaccio, a beach volleyball champion, developed his own strategy for making sure he practiced every day. He placed a volleyball just inside the door to his living room, so that when he walked into the house, he would see it. He had a stark choice: step over the ball or pick it up and start to practice. Most of the time he picked it up. His home will never win awards from a home decoration magazine, but he wasn't pursuing them. He was chasing a volleyball title. He got it.

"Success is neither magical nor mysterious," said motivational speaker Jim Rohn. "Success is the natural consequence of consistently applying basic fundamentals."

Your orange is your fundamental. It's a way of arranging and re-arranging your life to make room for greatness. It's a focus point to simplify your array of daily choices or to emphasize a necessary task. The correct orange ought to: make it more likely that you will practice, or make you more motivated to practice well, or create mental or physical fitness, or help you pay closer attention to the details of practice.

The correct orange becomes a crucial difference maker, something to set you apart not only from your competition but from your previous self.

It's a recognition that if you are to pursue real improvement, your preparation can't be ordinary. And with your orange, it won't be.

CHAPTER FOUR

Act Differently Than You Feel

"Your feelings are what you want. Your actions are what you get." -- **UNKNOWN**

One day in high school, my friend John stood over a physics lab table and said, "I don't feel like working today." After a pause, he added, "But I will work." With those words, he began his assignment. John wound up as our class valedictorian.

*** *** *** *** ***

At holiday time, people stand over a different kind of table. They gaze at the many desserts and say, "I know I shouldn't eat this. But I will."

*** *** *** *** ***

Your whole life depends on the relationship between your feelings and actions. Winners can separate the two. My friend John didn't feel like working, but he worked. He acted differently than he felt, and achieved great things. The people at the table put their feelings and actions together. They felt like eating, so they ate. They gained weight and felt guilty about it.

These two examples are not about whether you're a good person or a bad one. They're about a fact. Everyone has feelings, and everyone has days when they don't feel like practicing. If you can practice when you don't feel like it, you will improve more than people who don't. That's fact. Nothing personal. The grass is green, the sky is blue and winners practice when they don't feel like it.

*** *** *** *** ***

For years, my definition of work was just about the same as everyone else's. Work involved a lot of huffing and puffing. Then Jay Bilas, an ex-college basketball star and now a game analyst, wrote an article called "Defining Toughness in College Hoops." His premise was that too many players mistake trash-talking and chest-thumping for real toughness. Bilas listed several actions that he said showed real toughness on the basketball court.

His article made me think about my coaching. What exactly is hard work? Is it putting in more hours? Is it reading more books? What is it? To really improve at something, what must I do? My high school friend John knew. Real work is separating your feelings from your actions.

Michael Dell, who founded the computer company that bears his name, knows the difference between feelings and actions. "There are a lot of things that go into creating success," he said. "I don't like to do just the things I like to do. I like to do things that cause the company to succeed. I don't spend a lot of time doing my favorite activities."

*** *** *** *** ***

You can do what Dell does by the way you handle your actions and your feelings. You prove it every morning. You don't feel like getting up, but you do. Same way with going to work, going to the dentist, taking out the trash. You don't feel like it, but you do it. This ability to separate actions and feelings gives you great power over what you become.

You probably never thought of getting up in the morning as a form of power, but it is. It's the power that can help you practice and improve more than other people. It's the power that will make you get your raincoat when it rains out. It's the power that will vault you ahead of others who simply don't feel like it.

*** *** *** *** ***

Marathon champ Tom Fleming ran whether he felt like it or not. He discovered an extraordinary secret: As soon as he began to run, he began to feel like it. His actions changed his attitude. His motion changed his emotions. His movements changed his mood.

This happens to world-class athletes every day. They're constantly doing things they don't feel like doing. Do you honestly think that figure skaters enjoy getting up at 4 a.m. to practice? They do it anyway, and after a few spins around the ice, they're ready to get to work.

This one insight separates world-class performers from everyone else. They know that if you wait until you feel like doing something, you may never get started. If you start, you'll soon feel like it.

Remember: If you don't feel like practicing, just act differently than you feel!

CHAPTER FIVE

Park in the Right Lot

"It ain't what you don't know that gets you into trouble. It's what you know for sure that just ain't so." -- **MARK TWAIN**

If sports talk radio had existed in 1910, callers would have been screaming about Ty Cobb and Nap Lajoie. Both were among the best players in baseball, and they were battling for a prestigious prize: top batting average in the American League.

This average, known by all fans and used once upon a time by children to practice math, came from a simple calculation: the number of base hits divided by the number of times at-bat. In 1910, the race meant even more because the Chalmers Automobile Company was going to give the winner a car.

Day by day, newspapers and fans followed the chase. Adding to the frenzy was the contrast in personalities. People liked Lajoie and were rooting for him. Cobb was a wildly unpopular figure, so reviled that on the final day of the season an opposing manager cheated against him.

Even with the trickery, the race finished razor close, with opinions all around. Delighted with the buzz, Chalmers decided to give each player a car. Decades later, experts are still split on who won.

For all the furor, one question went unasked then and for long after: Exactly how much did batting average reflect a player's value to the team? Was it the best possible way to measure a player's performance? It turns out that the fans, the newspapers, Chalmers and just about everyone else were focusing on the wrong thing.

*** *** *** *** ***

Steve Jobs was never satisfied. It's what made him great (as well as tough to work for). He thought about things deeply. It took him and his wife eight years to pick out their furniture. They talked at dinner about what kind of washing machine would be best for their house. Even in the hospital with the disease that claimed his life, Jobs judged medical devices for size, shape, color and ease of use.

Author Malcolm Gladwell profiled Jobs in New Yorker magazine, asking this question: Was he a visionary or a tweaker? The answer? There's no question Jobs searched endlessly for a better way. "Steve Jobs," Gladwell wrote, "needed things to be perfect, and it took time to figure out what perfect was."

*** *** *** *** ***

One day I was running late for practice and was trying to get to the gym quickly. I pulled into the parking lot, hoping for an empty spot close to the door. Sure enough, there was one. It was a tight spot, requiring a sharp parking touch. Somehow, I pulled it off -- on the first try! I headed into the gym, patting myself on the back for saving a few seconds.

Then came the bad news. I was at the wrong gym. It was Wednesday, and on that day our team practices in the gym across town. I had forgotten, and it wound up costing me 10 more minutes, because I had to jump back into my car and go to our other gym.

Moral: It doesn't matter how well you park if you're not in the right lot. It doesn't matter if you do things right if you're not doing the right things.

*** *** *** *** ***

Caterina Fake is an award-winning mover and shaker on the Internet, having co-founded, among other things, the photo-sharing site Flickr. Fake says, "So often people work hard at the wrong thing. Working on the right thing is probably more important than working hard."

Amen.

The world is filled with poor strategies. In the 1950s, people who wanted to lose weight stood on a platform and placed a vibrating belt around their bellies. This was supposed to shake off the extra pounds. Fat chance. No matter how closely you followed the directions on the vibrating belt machine, it was never going to work. It was the wrong thing. Too bad the people using it never tried another strategy: Burn more calories than you consume.

Opinions change all the time. When I was a kid, it was a good thing to eat a hearty breakfast of bacon and eggs. Then eggs became bad for you. Now they're OK because the whites have protein. And the yolks have Omega-3s, so eating an egg now and then is somewhat good. Chocolate was bad, now dark chocolate is OK.

Remember those toe touches you did in high school gym? Probably not a great idea. And those neck rolls? Some people say they're dangerous.

It gets worse. When we learn and believe in something like the toe touches or the neck rolls or the eggs and bacon, we develop a bias about it. No one likes to be told that they're wrong.

"We tend to look for evidence to support our assumptions," someone once said. "Beware of self-deceiving observations and thoughts."

Amid all these opinions and biases, where can you find the best way to improve? Do you go by the latest fad? Something you saw on-line? Or is there something else?

There is something else, and it appeared to me years ago at a volleyball clinic in New Jersey. There, Dr. Carl McGown gave a life-changing talk to the coaches. Though he did not know us, he described our coaching journey as if he had been standing next to us in the gym.

"You've gone to coaching clinics," he began. Check. "You've watched videos." Check. "You've read books." Check. "You've spoken to other coaches." Check. "And lots of the information seemed to contradict itself." Check!

With that sentence, Dr. McGown had my full attention. In a world filled with bad information and poor strategies, how could you figure out the best way to do anything?

Principles, said Dr. McGown. Eternal truths. Things that do not change. He said it that day, and at many Gold Medal Squared coaching clinics since then. Here are four things about practice that never change.

1. Specificity. The practice should be as game-like as possible. If you want to improve at public speaking, practice in front of an audience. If you're trying to get better at basketball, then play basketball. Not everyone does this. Some basketball coaches, for example, teach their players to practice dribbling while they juggle a

tennis ball. Unfortunately, this never happens in a real game. A better use of time would be to dribble while being aware of people and movements on the court, because that's what the game is about.

2. Easy to hard. You never begin practice with difficult skills. You begin with easy ones, then work your way up. Master golf teacher Harvey Penick said that you should start every practice with four-foot putts and proceed from there. Make sure you are working just beyond your comfort zone. As soon as you do well on the four-foot putts, move farther from the hole.

3. Practice short and smart. Cramming may have worked in college, but it's not the best way to build skill. Here's the rule: It's better to do a little a lot than a lot a little. To get in great shape, work out every day instead of all day Saturday. Same way with juggling, violin, writing or selling, anything you can imagine. Study every day; don't cram. When UCLA was winning the basketball championship every year, Coach John Wooden practiced for only 90 minutes a day.

4. Feedback. Winners pay attention to results and decide what adjustments to make on the next try. Famous comedian George Burns used the simple feedback of audience laughter. If people laughed at a joke, it would stay in the act. If they didn't, the joke would get tossed out. Before long, the act was full of jokes that made the audience roar.

Taken together, these principles add up to something called "deliberate practice." This kind of practice involves giving attention to the task, with well-designed activities, meaningful repetitions and lots of feedback. That is the wisdom of the ages, confirmed by modern research.

Even guided by these principles, you must go on a journey of discovery to learn the best way to improve at what you do. You can't be like the baseball world of 1910, which was fascinated by, and rewarded, the wrong thing. You can't be like me, spending time in the wrong parking lot. You must be like Steve Jobs, endlessly looking for a better way.

*** *** *** *** ***

Years after Cobb and Lajoie were dead, a man came along, looking for a career. His name was Bill James, and he was just out of the Army. He worked nights at a pork and beans factory in the Midwest, but knew his future wasn't there. He did love baseball, and at work, he began to write down some thoughts about the game.

It turns out that James had a knack for asking thought-provoking questions. He was always wondering if there was a better way. He also had the follow-through to research the answers. James soon published his conclusions, though at first not many people paid attention.

Eventually, people would pay lots of attention. Because the questions James asked revolved mainly around one issue: Which statistics were truly most important? Which ones told exactly how valuable a baseball player was? These questions came at a crucial time in baseball history, because salaries were skyrocketing, and teams were competing for the best players. Before investing millions in a contract, the teams wanted to know exactly how valuable that player was.

Here was James, in a pork and beans factory, working on the answer. One question in particular interested him: Is batting average the best way to measure a batter's value? James came up with an opinion. His answer was no. Batting average was definitely not the best way to measure value. On-base percentage was much more important. For a century, the baseball world had been focusing on the wrong thing.

*** *** *** *** ***

Imagine you are a NASA scientist who wants to learn something about outer space. You have only so much money to spend. Your rocket can carry only so many instruments. You must be very careful to ask yourself, "How can I get the most science out of the resources I have?"

Your practice time is exactly the same. It comes down to "Now that I've decided to spend this next hour in practice, what is the best possible way to spend that hour?"
Suppose you're a baseball player trying to become a better hitter. You can ask yourself questions like these:

* What will batting practice look like?
* Should I take practice swings with weights on my bat?
* Should I hit off a tee?
* How much?
* Should I hit against a pitcher?
* How much?
* What exercises, if any, should I do when I'm not swinging a bat?

In other words, what is the best way to maximize the available time? What's the best way to do anything? That is your journey of discovery. Make sure you're in the right parking lot.

CHAPTER SIX

Review Your Goals Daily

"The human race is faced with a cruel choice: work or daytime television." **-- UNKNOWN**

On June 18, 1914, Lawrence Sperry acted like a boy showing off on a roller-coaster. He rode with his hands up in the air. He rode after climbing out of his seat. Those watching from the ground were struck with awe, because Sperry wasn't riding on a roller-coaster. He was flying a plane. His act would change history and save countless lives, because he had just invented the automatic pilot.

*** *** *** *** ***

Years ago, a baseball player named Jackie Brandt asked some teammates if they wanted to go out for ice cream. They said no when Brandt told them that the parlor was 30 miles away. Brandt won them over by saying that the shop had 28 different flavors. They hopped in the car and drove the 30 miles. When they got there, Brandt jumped out of the car ... and ordered vanilla.

*** *** *** *** ***

You live in the same world as Jackie Brandt and Lawrence Sperry do. There are so many choices, so many chances to go off course. You need something to keep you moving in the right direction. You need an automatic pilot, something to tell you where to direct your focus and energy.

That's why reviewing your goals every day can make all the difference. Doing so will remind you where you want to go, guiding the decisions you make all day long. Every time you face a decision, you can ask, "Will this get me closer to my goals or farther away?"

Goals simplify life. They lead you through the chaos. The sharper your goals, the simpler the road. Someone once said, "When one bases his life on principle, 99 percent of his decisions are already made."

This is certainly true when it comes to improvement. Reviewing your goals can help you with decisions like:

* Will I practice today?
* When will I start and how long will I continue?
* How hard will I work?

Trouble is, most people don't check in with their goals often enough. Peak performance coach Dave Cross of "Yes, I Can!" sports says that the No. 1 reason people don't reach their goals is they lose sight of them. People begin with great intentions but get distracted by errands, emergencies and other priorities. The more often you check your goals, the less these distractions will matter.

Famed Olympic decathlete Milt Campbell gives motivational talks, and asks his audiences about shaping their future. First he asks how many people have set goals. Many people raise a hand. Then Campbell asks how many have written down their goals. Not quite as many people can say yes to this one. Probing deeper, Campbell wants to know, "How many of you have your goals with you right now?" By that time, not many people are raising their hands.

Finally, Campbell asks about one more level: Have you checked your goals today? If you have, you are well ahead of 99 percent of the population, and you will be better equipped to manage the decisions you make every minute.

Without that daily check, you go off course. A wise person once said, "In absence of clearly defined goals, we become strangely loyal to performing daily acts of trivia."

You can decide exactly how you plan to keep your goals front and center. It could be through habits, reminders, rituals. You could take the example of my high school volleyball team, which won the state title by using a picture.

In the middle of a discouraging season, one of my players gave me a gift. It was an empty picture frame. She explained that even though the frame was empty at that moment, we would eventually fill it in with a picture of our state championship.

At that moment, the idea of winning anything -- much less a title -- seemed as far away as the moon. Still, I put it in the bookcase, a place where I would see it every day. Soon a picture formed in my mind. In the picture, our players were sprawled on the gym floor, crowded around a trophy. Weeks later, we won the championship. Someone took our picture, and the picture looked just like the one we had imagined.

You can use this technique. Just buy an empty frame and place it where you are sure to see it many times each day. Don't worry if the picture doesn't form in your mind right away. That can take time. If you like, you can put a picture in the frame. Some salesmen insert a picture of a car or of a vacation destination to remind them what their commissions can buy.

Your imagination will help you come up with more ways to keep your goals in front of you. Some suggestions:

One, you can write down your goals and carry them in your wallet. Then, just as John Vill'Neuve ate an orange first thing every day, you can check your goals at breakfast.

Two, follow the example of a young baseball player who kept his father's baseball card in his back pocket to remind him how much he wanted to follow in his father's footsteps. It need not be a baseball card; it could be a photo, a newspaper clip or any object that connects you with a vision of your future.

Three, you can make it a point to speak every day with someone who shares your wish to achieve. You can support and motivate each other.

In all of these cases, the constant contact keeps you from drifting. You stay focused while your competitors are jumping from one priority to another.

To see how quickly focus can shift, think about a doctor's waiting room. If there's a TV set, everyone starts watching the screen, even if it's a commercial or something they ordinarily would not watch. The TV was not on their minds when they entered. But it became a priority.

For an even more vivid example, look at commercials on TV. In a 30-second ad, the image can change as often as 25-30 times. That's because the producers believe that the audience has a short attention span. They keep the commercial moving.

Whether it's the doctor's office or watching TV, you can be different from other people. You can keep your focus while others lose theirs. Reviewing your goals every day will help.

How you remind yourself isn't nearly as important as doing it every day. There's the story of the Olympic figure skater who found it hard to wake up for practice early in the morning. She got a picture of her arch-rival and put it next to her bed. She also wrote the words, "While you were sleeping, I was practicing."

The more specific your goals, the greater effect they will have on your daily behavior. If you say, "I want to run a marathon," that will guide your actions only so far. If you say, "I want to run next year's Boston Marathon," the link between goals and action becomes more urgent. If you say, "I want to run next year's Boston Marathon in less than three hours," your daily decisions grow all the more sharp.

Let's say that you've committed to running the Boston Marathon in less than three hours. You've never done it in less than 3:10, but, then again, you've never practiced a daily review of your goals. This time you have a paper with 2:59:30 written in red, taped on your bathroom sink. This helps you with your decision on whether to run on those mornings when it's cold or wet. You have a similar paper placed near the television set as a reminder that if you waste too much time watching TV at night, it will be harder to wake up and run in the morning. Finally, you can place a third piece of paper on the refrigerator in case you must make some crucial decisions about what you eat.

These reminders can reinforce each other. With their help, you can enter the zone that Thomas Edison had in mind when he said, "If we did all the things we are capable of, we would literally astound ourselves."

What Edison was to inventing, the Montreal Canadiens were to hockey championships. In the 15 seasons from 1965 through 1979, the Canadiens won the Stanley Cup -- representing the National Hockey League championship -- 10 times. Some of those victories came from the inspiration they saw every day in their locker room. On the wall is a line from the poem "In Flanders Fields." It reads: "To you with failing hands we throw the torch, be yours to hold it high!" Within those words are contained the team goal: Win the Stanley Cup. These words beckon to every player who enters the room for the first time.

Team mottos can have the same effect. Written on a wall or on the back of a shirt, the right message can inspire and deepen tradition. But there are two important cautions. First, the message must come from within, especially in a team situation. A message imposed by a coach won't have the same effect as a sentiment that comes from within the team. Second, you've got to make sure the words don't just blend into the scenery. Goals work best if they are consciously reviewed.

Finally, use the pillow test to wrap up your day. When your head hits the pillow at night, you will either be saying, "I wish I had," or "I'm glad I did." In other words, did you do anything to move your goals forward that day, or did you let the day go by without the correct action? Knowing that you face that test every night can keep you focused on the right choice, whether it's a flavor of ice cream or a trip to the gym.

CHAPTER SEVEN

Finish Something

"I don't design clothes, I design dreams." -- **RALPH LAUREN**

On Oct. 28, 1965, Bill Quigley sat in a derrick, nearly 630 feet above the ground. His job was to place the final section of the St. Louis Arch into place, and the prospect had him shaking.

You could hardly blame Quigley for his case of nerves. Riding on his skilled hands were 30 years of planning and dreaming, millions of dollars and an untold measure of civic pride. For two and a half years, crews had pushed two separate legs toward the sky, with the hope they would meet and form an architectural masterpiece. Each new section they put into place required an error of no more than one-sixty-fourth of an inch, otherwise the project would fail. Workers measured at night to avoid the heat distortion of the sun.

Now it was time to see if everything worked. Below, a crowd of dignitaries and ordinary citizens watched. Helicopters flew overhead. Hydraulic jacks began to push the legs apart so the final section could fit. Firemen applied water to the south leg to cool it and put it back in alignment. Quigley, operating from the north tower, dropped the final piece into place. In later years, he joked that if he had botched the job, history would never have forgotten.

He didn't botch anything. The final section fit. The Arch was finished. Steamboats up and down the Mississippi River blew their whistles to celebrate.

Despite the doubts of those who thought the structure would buckle, despite the fact that when architect Eero Saarinen conceived it the technology to build it did not even exist, despite insurance actuaries' prediction that 13 men would lose their lives during the construction (none did), the project was finished.

"I think it represented, in a sense, the last out of a ballgame," park engineer Woody Zenfell said in the documentary film, "The Gateway Arch: A Reflection of America."

St. Louisans who had known the area could not fail to notice the difference, and not just because a structure now soared 630 feet into the air. The entire area around the Arch was transformed. No longer was it a collection of parking lots. It was now a national monument, an international destination that brought a sense of pride. Everything was different now: the horizon, the landscape, the mood. This is what completion does. It carries the power to transform and to fundamentally change.

*** *** *** *** ***

William James, commonly referred to as The Father of American Psychology, said, "Nothing is so fatiguing as the eternal hanging on of an uncompleted task."

David Lloyd George, the statesman who led the British Empire through World War I, put it this way: "There is nothing so fatal to character as half-finished tasks."

Yet life is littered with them. Unkept promises, broken resolutions and abandoned projects fill the landscape of our lives. People don't intend it to be that way. They want to do things. They plan to do things. It's just that they never do.

Sir Winston Churchill said: "It's not enough that we do our best; sometimes we have to do what's required."

Ed Smith, international best-selling author, produces a daily e-mail he calls the One-Minute Motivator. One of the most important messages he ever sent concerned reverence for the task. I don't know if Ed wrote this himself or was quoting someone else's wisdom, but it went like this: "Treat each task you do as the most important thing you have to do. Poorly executed tasks have a way of coming back to you. They undercut other people's confidence in you and they undercut your own self-confidence and pride. Turn off the cell phone and start taking things seriously."

John Stephen Ahkwari took finishing very seriously. In 1968, he was running the marathon in the Mexico City Olympics. Bloody and exhausted, he staggered past the finish line about 90 minutes after the winner did. When asked by disbelieving witnesses why he kept going, Ahkwari said, "My country did not send me 5,000 miles to start a race, they sent me to finish it."

What Ahkwari is to marathon lore, Jean-Dominique Bauby was to writing books. Bauby, onetime editor of "Elle" magazine, suffered a stroke and was left unable to move any part of his body except his eyelids. Using only his ability to blink, and with someone else writing it down, Bauby wrote the masterpiece "The Diving Bell and the Butterfly."

The book required about 200,000 blinks to write and an average word took about two minutes. Each of those blinks, each of those words, represented a chance for Bauby to get frustrated, to get tired, to quit. He kept blinking. He died less than two weeks after the book was published.

Tennis great Martina Navratilova is also a finisher. She showed it in the many events she won, and she even showed it as a contestant on the reality show "I'm a Celebrity ... Get Me Out of Here." She had to deal with cockroaches and bizarre stunts, but never quit. "It was a challenge," she said. "And once I sink my teeth into something, I want to finish it." Navratilova is more than someone who finishes things. She is someone who is in the HABIT of finishing things.

*** *** *** *** ***

Unfinished jobs are more than just loose ends from your past. They affect everything you're doing now. They distract you with some vague sense of something not quite right. They hurt your confidence, because it's hard to believe in someone -- especially yourself -- who keeps breaking promises. Finally, as park engineer Woody Zenfell suggested in comparing the last piece of the Arch to the last out of a ballgame, winning and finishing go hand and hand. You can't win without finishing. You can't win a race without crossing the finish line. Winners not only complete their work, they win BECAUSE they complete their work.

If you are going to improve, you must develop a world-class approach to finishing. Whether you're building an arch, or running a marathon or writing a book blink by blink, you must make finishing a habit. Here are some ways to become a world-class finisher.

Finish something within 15 minutes of getting up in the morning. Perhaps it's eating an orange, or reviewing your goals or doing some exercise. To develop even more finishing power, develop a to-do list the night before. Be very careful about what you write down on that list. If the task is important enough to put on your list, it is important enough to finish. Every task you finish will add to your confidence, and every task you do not finish will hurt it.

By combining the 15-minute rule with a careful selection of tasks, you can quickly become more skilled at finishing things. There will be fewer broken promises littering the landscape of your life.

Two, decide on your standards. It's not enough just to do things; it's important to do them right. If you do a task poorly, it's just as bad as not finishing. Jim Slater, a friend from my sports writing days, once told me how impressed he was by a visit to a gas station in Watertown, NY. He pulled in and received full service: windshield cleaning, tire check, oil and fluid check. All this service came with a smile, even though the weather was brutally cold. The gas station attendant had decided that this was the standard, no matter what the weather.

Three, ask yourself if what you are doing is having an effect. This is critical to practice, where if you do not accomplish something you have wasted your time. Helen Keller said, "I long to accomplish a great and noble task, but it is my chief duty to accomplish small tasks as if they were great and noble." If you do not accomplish something in practice, then you have practiced not finishing things.

View every practice as a project, just like the St. Louis Arch. It needs completion, just like the Arch did. Unfortunately, it was a lot easier for people to judge whether the Arch was finished than for people to know whether or not their practice has been successful. Often there is no magic "final section" in practice. How do you know if, after you have put in the time, you have actually built strength, agility, skill or understanding?

45

Measurement

When you're trying to improve at something, nothing beats clear evidence that you're getting better. Let's say you're a weekend golfer trying to improve the quality of your practice. You've decided to take the advice of master teacher Harvey Penick and start your session by trying to make four-foot putts.

The first time, you make six out of 10 from that range. The second time, you make eight out of 10. The third time, you make nine out of 10, including seven in a row. You're clearly getting better! Your practice is having an effect!

Then, after making your four-foot putts, you increase the putting distance to five feet. The first time, you make three out of 10. The second time, you make five out of 10. You have now raised both your performance AND the degree of difficulty. There is no doubt that you have improved. Your practice has had an effect.

If you can jump a little higher today than you did a month ago, or if you can lift more weight, or if you can make more consecutive free throws, you get a tangible connection between your work and your results. Anything that shows progress will motivate you to work hard. It will also validate your effort and approach to practice.

Feedback

Here's a definition of feedback: It's information about the past that you can use in the present to improve your future. Your four-foot putts can give you at least four forms of feedback.

1. Result. This is the path of the ball. It either goes into the hole, or it goes left, or it goes right, or it is short. The

information is there for you. Many people miss this feedback because they get frustrated over a bad result. There is a point in every practice when feedback gives you a choice: You can either become frustrated by the result or fascinated by the problem. Winners become fascinated. When the ball goes to the left of the hole, they will make an adjustment and aim their next ball slightly to the right. By this process of trial and error, they will improve.

2. Knowledge of performance. This often is input from a coach. Performers sometimes do not know what their body is doing while performing a skill. They need help from a trusted outside observer. A good golf practice might focus on keeping the head down during the stroke. A good coach will give constant feedback. "Yes, you kept your head still" or "No, you looked up." In the best practices, the performer will see a link between improved result (where the ball goes) and improved technique (keeping the head down). Players can also get knowledge of performance from video.

3. Goals. Remember Ralph Lauren's quote about designing dreams? You can, too. In fact, good design is vital to improvement. You must begin your session with a vision of where you want to be at the end. You need a goal, and the more vivid the better. The story of swimmer Florence Chadwick shows how important it is to hold a vision in the mind. She tried an historic swim from Catalina Island to the California coast. During her trip, a fog set in, making it impossible for her to see the coast. Without a vision of the target, she quit. She was crestfallen to learn that the shore was only a mile away. She learned from the experience and tried again two months later. This time when the fog set in, Chadwick held a mental picture of the coastline, and she succeeded in her swim. This technique can make all the difference in your practices.

4. Finally, there are measured repetitions. Measure as many things as you can during practice. This will build

intensity and make you more accountable. A numerical goal can do for you what the vision of the shore did for Florence Chadwick. Not only can it keep you focused and working hard, it gives you satisfaction when you reach it.

To really be a finisher, use feedback after practice. Take some time to see if you've accomplished what you intended. Did you make progress? If not, why not? Was it because of a flawed plan? Or was it because of poor effort? Perhaps there were too many distractions. Whatever the reason, taking a look at your just-finished practice can help you with the next one.

You can see elements of deliberate practice in the St. Louis Arch. It began with a vision, then progressed to blueprints. As the legs went skyward, feedback took place in the form of the daily measurements needed to keep them aligned. This model of seeing the goal, performing the action, then correcting the result is guaranteed to make your practice sessions meaningful.

More than anything, finishing becomes a matter of attitude. Only you can decide whether or not you will see things through. When you finish, you separate yourself from your foes. You can adopt that attitude right now. One day Francis of Assisi was hoeing his garden. Someone asked what he would do if he learned he would die before sunset. He replied, "I would finish hoeing my garden."

CHAPTER EIGHT

Be Present

"Let us not look back in anger, nor forward in fear, but around in awareness." **-- JAMES THURBER**

On Sept. 21, 2001, Mike Piazza came to bat in a big-league baseball game. A veteran of 10 seasons, Piazza had done this thousands of times. This night was different. This was the first baseball game in New York after a terror attack destroyed the Twin Towers. In the stands were 41,235 people who desperately needed a diversion from the shock and horror of the preceding 10 days.

Now it was the eighth inning, and the Mets were behind the Atlanta Braves by one run. Piazza swung at a pitch from Steve Karsay and hit it deep into the night for a home run. As he trotted around the bases, those fans stood and yelled out a celebration. For the first time in 10 days, there was a sense of normalcy; the recovery had begun.

Few, if any, of those fans had noticed what Piazza had done in the few moments before he came to the plate. He had paused to breathe.

*** *** *** *** ***

Michael Irvin, a Hall of Fame football player, was once a contestant on the television show "Dancing With the Stars." After one of his performances, Irvin was asked by the host whether his score was higher or lower than he had expected. After a long pause, Irvin replied, "I'm just here."

Think about that.

"I'm just here."

*** *** *** *** ***

Both Irvin and Piazza are trying to strip away all the non-essentials. Irvin can't worry about what the judges say or do; all he can do is dance to the best of his ability. Piazza can't afford to think of the score, the crowd or anything except hitting the ball. Piazza, with his breathing, and Irvin, with his desire to be "just here," are trying to accomplish the same thing: be present in a very special way.

For those hoping to improve, being in the present represents one of the toughest challenges.

A 2010 study conducted by Harvard University showed that people spend nearly half of their waking hours not thinking about what they are actually doing. The study, conducted via the iPhone, indicated that people spent 46.9% of their waking hours with their minds wandering.

One of the researchers, Dr. Matthew Killingsworth, said: "This study shows that our mental lives are pervaded, to a remarkable degree, by the non-present."

The non-present is the enemy of improvement. Regret over the past, and anxiety about the future, are killers. Only the present matters, and here's a special team exercise I've done to emphasize that. I place a chair in the middle of the huddle, then call for a volunteer. "Pick up the chair," I tell the volunteer. The player picks up the chair. Then I say, "Pick up the chair yesterday." The player giggles, not knowing what to do. She can't do what we ask. That's the point. You can't do anything yesterday or tomorrow. You can only act in the present.

For centuries, man has struggled with the challenge of living in the present. Euripides said, "Waste not fresh tears over old griefs." Today's pace has only made the challenge harder. We are trying to do many things. We rush from place to place and from experience to experience, without any chance to absorb. Most of the time there is not a minute to reflect, much less practice.

If you want to improve, this must change. You must take time to think about what you are doing or, as sports psychologist Dr. Rob Gilbert says, to "keep your mind on what you are doing while you are doing it." You must be present physically, mentally and emotionally. You must practice the way you watched the most spell-binding movie you ever saw: with full absorption. Here's how.

First, pay attention. Your teachers in school were right. Paying attention is not just something they said to make you stop fidgeting. It is the key to gaining skill. Dr. Anders Ericsson, the world's leading figure on expert performance, has written that the most important condition for improved performance is "the subjects' motivation to attend to the task and exert effort to improve ..." In other words, pay attention! Knowing this, believing this and taking it to heart makes a difference in the way you approach practice.

Second, breathe. Piazza was truly inspired with his approach to hitting. When asked what he did when he was awaiting his turn at bat, Piazza replied, "I gain control of my breathing." No one could have said or done it better. What breathing does, more than anything else in a busy world, is put you in the present. Nothing is more immediate. You can go for days without eating, sleeping or drinking, but you won't last very long without breathing. The very act of stopping to pay attention to your breathing will slow things down and bring them to their core.

You can raise the level of your practices with this principle. Start by using breathing as a punctuation mark. Use it to separate what just happened from what is about to happen. Use it to separate your frantic daily pace from the deliberate, conscious effort that you will exert in practice.

Just before practice, gain control of your breathing. Think of nothing else. Concentrate on your inhale and exhale. Breathe out the bad thoughts and breathe in power and energy. The more deeply you breathe, the more firmly you will be in the present. Once you're deeply into your breathing, think of why you have come to practice. Think of what you are there to accomplish.

Once you get good at this warmup, you can add a feature. Compile a movie of all your past successes. Put everything in there: your schoolwork, your sports, your theater, anything at which you have enjoyed a shining moment. After you gain control of your breathing, start running this movie in your mind. See yourself at your best. Get involved in this movie, just as you would get totally wrapped up in your favorite TV show.

Combine the breathing with affirmations. An affirmation is a phrase or statement underlining your ideal self. Golfer Phil Mickelson used this technique to finally capture a major championship. Entering the Masters Tournament in 2004, Mickelson owned an unfortunate reputation as the greatest golfer never to have won a major title. But in the final round of that tournament, when the pressure was greatest, he began to say to himself, "Today is my day." Through good shots and bad, he repeated those words. They kept him firmly in the present. Every time he was tempted to regret something or worry about something, he stayed centered with those simple words. Sure enough, he won. An affirmation, combined with deep breathing, makes a powerful combination to keep you in the present.

Finally, just before you begin practice, take one large exhale. This is a gesture to your body and mind that something special is about to happen. It feels good, relaxes the muscles and calms the heart.

Once practice begins, breathe whenever you get a chance to pause and attempt a crucial skill. Basketball players do it just before shooting free throws. Olympians in a wide range of sports do it.

To really set yourself apart, let breathing keep you centered in moments of failure. Most of your competitors get distracted and overwhelmed when they fail at something. They feel embarrassed or inadequate, and these feelings get in the way of doing what most needs to be done: learning and trying again. At moments of failure, if you pause and breathe, you can re-center yourself on the task. You will be doing that crucial extra that others are not doing.

*** *** *** *** ***

Pat Summitt, coach of the Tennessee women's basketball team, uses a basic technique to keep her players in the present. She demands that they look her in the eye. It's not just a casual look. Summitt has a penetrating stare that locks onto the player's eyes. At that moment, it is hard for the player to think about anything except the present.

Giants football coach Tom Coughlin uses a similarly simple technique. At team meetings, he insists that his players sit up straight, with no slouching. It seems like a kindergarten exercise, but it is powerful to the core. No one can be sure if Coughlin's players are really listening. At least they act like they are listening.

*** *** *** *** ***

Use your senses to stay in the present. For instance, look at the sky. Do you remember a day when you lay down in the grass, stared up at the sky and just looked at the clouds? Remember how refreshing and absorbing that was? Dr. Ann Rasmussen, a psychologist, recommends bringing those days back now and then. She lays it out beautifully in describing what the sky can do:

"Its vastness humbles us and reorients us to how petty some preoccupations are. Its stark and ever-changing beauty refocuses our eyes. We shift our breathing from shallow and fretful to expanded and peaceful. We get over ourselves, out of ourselves, revitalized and re-heartened."

In other words, a simple look at the sky can make you feel better. It helps you breathe; it puts things in perspective; it energizes; it refreshes. This is especially important during the daily grind of a season or of study. Without a change of scenery, you become a candidate for burnout. An occasional look at the sky, at its beauty and its possibilities, can help you avoid that.

While you're at it, take some time to listen. Too often we pay no attention to the background noise in life. Oh, we'll listen to music or TV shows, but seldom to birds, wind or the hum of the highway. Do you know why winter wind sounds different than summer wind? It's because in summer there are leaves that rustle. In the winter, there is only the harshness of the branches. Listening puts you in the present and calms the mind.

Sometimes a laugh will do wonders for your practice. When Tommy Lasorda was managing the Los Angeles Dodgers, he would bring in comedian Don Rickles to loosen up the clubhouse. Rickles, whose specialty was insults, spared no one. By the time he finished his monologue, everyone was laughing, and it was hard for anyone to have too much of an ego.

Whether it's looking at the sky or pausing to listen or having a good laugh, you want to enjoy the journey. It's important to pursue your goals with joy, not with grimness. When great coaches reflect, they don't point to victories. They point to moments, and to people. They have found things to enjoy each day.

In 1979, the Pittsburgh Pirates won the World Series. Not only did they have star players, they also discovered how to bond and enjoy the season. They adopted as their team anthem a hit song of the day: Sister Sledge's disco hit "We Are Fam-i-ly." On the day the Pirates won the National League pennant, assuring themselves of a trip to the World Series, their wives were dancing on the top of the dugout. There was nothing grim about that team!

Finally, as Dr. Ericsson says, true deliberate practice is all about staying in the present. It requires attention to the task, attention to the feedback and renewed attention to the next attempt. If you can, in Ericsson's words, "attend to task and exert effort," then you will be in the present and improve.

Deliberate practice -- with its focus on task, its many repetitions and its constant feedback -- is extremely demanding, so make sure you take steps to enjoy the journey. Look at the sky and get absorbed in the shape of the clouds. Laugh. Listen to the summer and winter winds. Adopt a song. Smile. Take time to breathe.

Perhaps most importantly, take time each day to congratulate yourself on the quest you have chosen. There is no joy or glory in small achievements. It takes courage to traffic in great themes, and you are doing it. Great surfers test the greatest waves; mountain-climbers look to Mount

Everest. Poet Rainer Maria Rilke captured this sense of great themes in "The Man Watching." It goes, part,

"What we choose to fight is so tiny!
What fights us is so great!
If only we would let ourselves be dominated
as things do by some immense storm,
we would become strong too ..."

Do more than respect your rivals; love and appreciate them. Without them, you would have no way of proving your greatness. You would have no way to test yourself and to bring out the best in yourself.

As I write this, I think of the New York Yankees, the University of Connecticut women's basketball team, the University of North Carolina women's soccer squad, all teams that set the gold standard for excellence. By being that great, these teams are inviting others to be stronger, faster and tougher. For those teams that have accepted this invitation, there is now a journey. I hope that they are enjoying it, moment by moment, by staying in the present and making that present full and productive.

CHAPTER NINE

Focus on Your Focus

"Concentrate all your thoughts upon the work at hand." --
ALEXANDER GRAHAM BELL

The stakes were as hard and cold as the ice.

If the Vancouver Canucks won this Stanley Cup playoff
game, they would remain alive in their series and play a
Game 6. If they lost, their hockey season – and any dreams
of a championship – would end.

So here they were, playing the Anaheim Mighty Ducks in
sudden death overtime. The first team to score would win.
It's an unforgiving format that allows no mistakes.

Defending the goal for Vancouver was Roberto Luongo.
No one had done more to keep his team in the game than
Luongo had. The Canucks had been outplayed for most of
the evening, but he stopped more than 50 shots while
allowing only one goal.

Now the teams entered a second overtime period, with
score 1-1 and the tension growing ever higher. Suddenly, in
the 25th minute of overtime, a collision took place to
Luongo's right. He thought a teammate had been fouled,
and he expected the referee to call a penalty. When that did
not happen, Luongo momentarily raised his arms in protest.

In that one instant when Luongo wasn't concentrating on
his job, the puck came to Scott Niedermayer of the Ducks,
who shot it into the goal to end the game. Just like that, the

season was over for the Canucks. Anaheim not only won the series, but went on to win the championship.

In a post-game interview, Luongo explained the lapse that ended a dream. "I thought there was an elbow (penalty), so I looked at the ref for one split-second and when I turned my head, the puck was coming at me," he said.

One split-second of lost focus. That's all it took to make the difference between victory and defeat.

Your life and your work are a lot like Roberto Luongo's. When you focus properly, your chances of success go up. When your focus weakens, they go down. It doesn't matter whether you're playing in the National Hockey League or trying to make the high school varsity.

Tennis great Martina Navratilova says, "I just try to concentrate on concentrating."

Baseball superstar Alex Rodriguez has said his top goal is to concentrate fully for an entire game. No word on whether he's ever succeeded.

To fully appreciate the role of focus in your success, it helps to understand three things: First, focus is science. It's not just something your coaches like to nag you about. It's something that's real and powerful. Second, no matter what anybody has ever said, you have an incredible ability to focus. Third, most people take this incredible ability and focus on the wrong thing.

The Science of Focus

Daniel Bernoulli was born in 1700, long before anyone ever flew in a plane. Yet his work helps explain why airplanes fly and how you can develop great skill.

Bernoulli studied air and liquids, and he described a principle that was named after him. It says: The faster air (or fluid) moves, the lower its pressure. Planes fly because the pressure under their wings is greater than the pressure on top. Your shower curtain billows in because the water in the shower creates low pressure.

What does this have to do with you? Everything. Let's change the sentence a little bit.

Instead of saying: "The faster air moves, the lower its pressure," we could say, "The faster the attention moves, the lower its effect."

In his book "Five Equations That Changed the World," Michael Guillen uses the example of a receiving line at a political dinner. The politician moves quickly through the line, greeting each guest, until he comes to someone who has donated a large sum of money. That's when the politician slows down and spends lots of time with that special donor. He wants to have a big effect.

According to this principle, if you rush through your homework, you will learn less. If you move more slowly through your homework, you learn more. Same thing with acquiring skill on piano. The more time and care you take with your practice, the more effect you will have. This is not opinion, or the peppy words of a motivational speaker. It is science. This special time you take with your practice is the proper focus that champions need.

Your Incredible Ability to Focus

Have you ever spent an entire day waiting for something special? Maybe it was a game, or a concert or a trip to an amusement park. On days like this, you showed an incredible focus. You carefully arranged your schedule. You made sure that nothing got in the way. You never let yourself become distracted.

Every year in the middle of winter, millions of Americans prove their incredible ability to focus on problems -- and to solve them. They attend Super Bowl parties and then watch the game. Maybe it doesn't sound like much of a problem to watch the Super Bowl. But it is. On most days, unexpected things crop up to distract you from your plans. On Super Bowl Sunday, these things never seem to get in the way. People are determined to watch the game, and they make sure they do it. They form priorities, and they produce extra effort. They show that when they really want to, they can summon the focus necessary for success. To repeat: You have an incredible ability to focus.

Most People Focus on the Wrong Thing

One day my wife and I were out together, looking forward to dinner at a restaurant. While driving through town, we were pulled over by a policeman. When we asked what was the matter, he said, "You drove through a crosswalk while a pedestrian was entering. That man back there was a county detective. Did you see him?"

We had been caught in a sting. The detective stood on the curb, then stepped into the crosswalk. Any driver who drove through received a ticket for $130. It certainly ruined our dinner.

The next day I drove through that same section of town again. This time, my attitude changed. Instead of talking, or changing the radio station or looking at the storefronts, I was actually paying attention to the road.

At that moment, I realized what real focus was. It's not just concentrating hard. It's a way of life. It's deciding what you will pay attention to. I realized how easy it is to focus on the wrong thing. And how often people do it.

*** *** *** *** ***

Taken together, these three points about focus offer an astonishingly simple blueprint for you. Success becomes a matter of using your incredible power to focus, and constantly applying it to the right thing. This is harder than it looks. Why?

Let's start with Sherlock Holmes, who, even though he is a fictional character, can teach performers a lot about success. In the very first Holmes story, "A Study in Scarlet," Dr. Watson is just getting to know Holmes, when he makes a discovery about his new friend: He doesn't even know that the Earth revolves around the sun!

"You appear to be astonished," (Holmes) said. "Now that I do know it I shall do my best to forget it."

When Watson protests, Holmes says, "You say that we go round the sun. If we went round the moon it would not make a pennyworth of difference to me or to my work."

That passage explains one reason why people don't always focus on what they should: societal pressure. Watson was genuinely offended when Holmes admitted his ignorance of the solar system. Watson even said that a "civilized" person should know better. But Holmes wasn't interested in knowing a little bit about this and a little bit about that. He wanted to know everything about what concerned him.

Be like Holmes. Don't be well-rounded. Develop sharp edges. If you want to be world-class at one thing, you're going to have to leave lots of other things behind. Your focus will have to be incredibly narrow.

What's another reason why people focus on the wrong thing? They are human. They know they should eat well, but they are tempted by cheeseburgers. They know they should do homework, but they watch television instead. They know that they should give full effort to every single practice, but their minds wander.

In my sports writing days, I witnessed several examples of extraordinary focus. One came in a crucial hockey match involving Mike Bossy of the New York Islanders. Bossy was one of the top goal-scorers who ever lived. In this particular match came a moment where the goalie was caught way out of position. Bossy found himself alone in front of the net, with no one guarding him or the net. He calmly shot the puck into the open goal, and the Islanders won the game.

Afterwards, someone asked Bossy what he was thinking, alone in front of the net, with no one to bother him. Bossy replied, "I was thinking that if anything went wrong, it wouldn't be because I got careless."

What a mind! In that situation, some players might have celebrated too early and become careless. Not Bossy. His focus actually increased!

To summarize, it's not easy to focus on the right thing. There are distractions, as in Luongo's case. There will be pressure for you to become well-rounded. Finally, there's just human nature. Nevertheless, if you can find the right thing and focus on it, and do it all the time, you will achieve great success. That's not just talk. It's science.

CHAPTER TEN

Be on Guard Against the Self

"When life looks like Easy Street, there is danger at your door." -- **THE GRATEFUL DEAD**

In the summer of 1995, Greg Maddux was the best baseball pitcher in the world. He had already won the Cy Young Award as the league's top pitcher three years in a row, and he would win it again later that season.

Here he was on a Sunday afternoon, watching the Philadelphia Phillies take batting practice. Suddenly Maddux spied a player he didn't recognize, and he turned to baseball writer Rich Dubroff and asked who the player was. That one question made a deep impression on Dubroff.

"The night before, Maddux had pitched a masterpiece against this very same team," Dubroff recalled. "Twelve hours later, he was scouting hitters he didn't know because he might be facing them in the future. I've seen a couple of pitchers watch batting practice; but none as avidly as Maddux."

Maddux worked harder on the days when he DIDN'T pitch than most people worked on the day when they DID pitch. His work ethic helps explain why Maddux ranks as one of the greatest pitchers who ever lived. He managed to avoid the thing that sabotages success -- the feeling that you've arrived. He never gave in to complacency. He never got caught up in the awards, his accomplishments or his status as a superstar. He was always looking for any detail that could make him successful, while at the same time avoiding the pitfalls that come with success.

"Success is a ruthless competitor for it flatters and nourishes our weaknesses and lulls us into complacency," said Samuel Tilden, a politician of the 1800s.

Renowned golfer Bobby Jones put it this way: "The mark of a champion is to be everlastingly on the lookout against the self."

Ross Perot, Texas billionaire and two-time candidate for president, goes into beautiful detail on the dangers of success.

"Something in human nature...causes us to start slacking off at our moment of greatest accomplishment," Perot said. "As you become successful...you will need a great deal of self-discipline not to lose your sense of balance, humility, and commitment."

Aesop wrote about complacency more than 500 years B.C. in his fable "The Tortoise and the Hare." In it, the swift hare is racing the plodding tortoise. After building a huge lead, the hare goes to sleep. The tortoise keeps putting one foot ahead of the other. The hare awakens just in time to see the tortoise approach the finish line and, despite one last burst of speed, cannot recover the lost time.

Great performers behave the opposite way. They never let themselves get comfortable. Jackie Robinson, who broke baseball's color line, titled his autobiography, "I Never Had It Made." He never felt he could relax. Maybe that was his nature. More likely it was the fact that as the only African-American in big-league baseball, he was always on display and being tested.

Golfer Peter Jacobsen was acutely aware of this need to constantly prove oneself. "One of the most fascinating things about golf," he said, "is how it reflects the cycle of life. No matter what you shoot -- the next day you have to go back to the first tee and begin all over again and make yourself into something."

Great performers approach practice with a mixture of respect, humility, curiosity and hunger. There is a sense of desperation, and of a sense that time is short and success is fleeting.

Hockey Hall of Famer Bryan Trottier revealed this mindset during the 1980 Stanley Cup playoffs. His team, the New York Islanders, was playing its best hockey of the year. As the playoffs proceeded, it became increasingly likely that the Islanders could win the championship. A reporter asked Trottier how he felt.

"Scared," Trottier said. "I'm scared that I may wake up tomorrow and not be in the zone that I'm in now."

Trottier, then only 23 years old, showed uncommon wisdom in guarding his attitude. He knew how hard it was to reach a certain mental state, and he protected it with near-religious fervor. He knew he couldn't take it for granted.

"To live we must conquer incessantly," said Henri Frederic Amiel, a Swiss writer who defined charm as "the quality in others that makes us more satisfied with ourselves."

The hare in Aesop's fable, and the many performers who have failed through complacency, beg a maddening question: Why do people stop doing things that work for them? How can people practice so they avoid being the hare? It comes down to four words: respect, humility, hunger and curiosity. Those four words can be boiled down to one.

"Pietas" is a Latin word loosely translated as "piety." In ancient Rome, the word meant even more. It carried a sense of action and honor, and could be translated as "dutiful conduct, sense of duty, religiousness, devotion."

If you can practice with the word "pietas" in mind, you have reached a higher level of preparation. You have arrived at a point where the devotion to task is near sacred.

You can go about your work like Paul Erdos, a mathematician with an endless fascination with his field. He saw beauty in numbers, and published more than 1400 papers. Like an itinerant religious figure, he would show up at the doorsteps of colleagues and say, "My mind is open." He would help the colleague with a problem until it was solved. Then he would move on. He embodied the sense of never being satisfied. When you think of respect, hunger, humility and curiosity, you can think of Paul Erdos.

Respect

Pat Summitt, who has coached the University of Tennessee women's basketball team to eight national titles, places respect at the center of her program. Summitt has developed her "Definite Dozen," a system for achieving and sustaining success. First among the dozen is "Respect yourself and others." Summitt has said, "There is no such thing as self-respect without respect for others."

If respect begins with the self, it goes way beyond that. Respect extends to the equipment, the facility, the people who clean the facility and the entire process of getting better. As American operatic soprano Beverly Sills has observed, "There are no shortcuts to any place worth going." Football coach John Madden adds, "The road to Easy Street goes through the sewer."

As part of that respect, Summitt tells her players, "Sit up straight, listen and participate."

Humility

English playwright W. Somerset Maugham once said, "It wasn't until quite late in life that I discovered how easy it is to say 'I don't know!'"

He was not alone. Most people find it hard to admit they don't know. It is difficult for most people to admit any shortcoming whatsoever.

Baseball pioneer Branch Rickey was just the opposite. He was well aware of his limitations even though, as a baseball executive who helped build championships with three different teams, he was considered the greatest mind in the history of his sport.

Rickey was once asked how much baseball he knew, as opposed to how much baseball could be known. "Sixty-two percent," was his oddly precise answer. Was he correct? Who knows? What's important is that Rickey, despite being a venerated figure in his industry, felt there was a great deal he did not know about it.

So it is with the masters. If they can learn something, it doesn't matter whether the teacher is a guru or a beginner. Team-building expert Gary Pritchard was attending an obscure soccer lecture in an out-of-the-way meeting room in a hotel. He was astonished and delighted when a coach sat down next to him. It was Anson Dorrance, winner of 21 national titles at the University of North Carolina. Dorrance wanted to keep learning. Basketball great John Wooden did, too. He spent his off-seasons focusing on one area in which he felt he could improve.

Great leaders, and the athletes they coach, must approach life with a delicate balance. They work hard to achieve supreme confidence, all while retaining a sense of humility. They must perform like masters, but prepare like novices. They observe the samurai code: "With true strength comes humility."

Curiosity

Albert Einstein once observed, "I am no genius. I am merely very curious."

If Einstein was correct, then the vastness of the universe opens to all of us. Our intelligence quotient is not nearly as important as our interest quotient. Einstein truly was curious. He spent many hours wondering what it would be like to ride on a beam of light. His long hours of thought led to the Theory of Relativity.

Whether you're a coach or a performer, you have a choice: whether to be frustrated or fascinated. Great practice involves endless fascination with questions like these:

* What are the best things to do?
* What is the best way to do them?
* In what order should you do them?
* How long should you do them?
* How often should you do them?

Martina Navratilova found herself endlessly fascinated by tennis. "I love the game," she said. "It's a challenge to me, and it's interesting, it's intriguing, it's fascinating, and I always try to figure out how to do it better."

Great achievers are always looking for the best use of available time. They want to know if there is a better way. They live by the maxim "success leaves clues," and they study what other great performers do. They leave notebooks on their nightstand so they can jot down ideas that arrive in the middle of the night.

They are like one-year-olds, who want to touch and taste everything. They want to hear about new ideas, discuss them and try them. Their curiosity may sometimes send them on detours, but danger from their curiosity is nothing compared to the danger of leading an unexplored life.

Greg Mattison, defensive coordinator for the Baltimore Ravens, saw curiosity and hunger in linebacker Ray Lewis. Said Mattison: "He watches film like a coach and he listens like a rookie."

That sounds very much like the saying: Practice like you're the worst, play like you're the best.

<u>Hunger</u>

This was a late night in the composing room of The Star-Ledger in Newark, N.J. Sport editor Willie Klein looked at the statistics page for the next morning's paper. He judged it with a critical eye: Was the information correct? Was it up-to-date? Was it presented neatly? Was there any item that could be replaced with one that was more interesting? Klein thought there was room for improvement. He called upstairs to the copy desk, and told them to send more statistics.

This is how Willie Klein spent his last night on the job. It was New Year's Eve and, at age 81, he was wrapping up a 62-year career with the paper. On a night when no one would have faulted him for kicking back and letting others run the show, Klein was in the least glamorous room in the building, looking at the least glamorous page, trying to make tomorrow's paper just a little bit better.

"He was forever thankful that he had the job and would do anything to make sure it was done right," recalled Klein's son Moss, himself a newspaper man who took great care on the job. "He had a tremendous sense of responsibility."

Through 62 years, Klein never lost his hunger. On the last day of his career, he worked harder than the most ambitious beginner. How? Why? Who knows? Klein was like another New Jerseyan, Bruce Springsteen, who said it best in his song "Dancing in the Dark." "You gotta stay hungry."

In a 1961 interview with the New York Times, baseball Hall of Famer Joe DiMaggio said much the same as Springsteen would. "A ball player's got to be kept hungry to become a big-leaguer," DiMaggio said. "That's why no boy from a rich family ever made the big leagues."

Thinking along the same lines, aerospace businessman Norman Ralph Augustine said: "A hungry dog hunts best. A hungrier dog hunts even better."

Hunger is that certain something inside a person that keeps them wanting more. Some people have it, some people don't.

Said actor Johnny Depp: "For me, ambition is a dirty word. I prefer hunger. To be hungry -- great. To have hopes, dreams -- great."

CHAPTER ELEVEN

Be Extreme

"Here's to the crazy ones ... the round pegs in the square holes, the ones who see things differently. Because they change things. They push the human race forward." -- **JACK KEROUAC**

Niels Bohr never used computers in his day, but his work helped make sure we can use them in ours. Born in Denmark in 1885, Bohr grew up to win a Nobel Prize in physics. He studied the world of quantum mechanics, complete with ideas like time travel, multiple universes and particles that seem to be in two places at one time. Really crazy stuff.

No wonder he once famously exclaimed, presumably to a fellow scientist, "We all agree that your theory is crazy. But is it crazy enough?"

Like Bohr's work, his words can help you today. If you're really interested in getting better at what you do, you must ask yourself these questions: "Am I crazy enough? Is what I am doing crazy enough?"

Here's the reality if you want to improve more than others. You can't be ordinary. You can't do what other people do. Your habits, your approach, your focus, must all be extraordinary. Even if you do ordinary things, you must do them in a way that no one else will.

"There's nothing in the middle of the road but yellow stripes and dead armadillos," said Jim Hightower, an author and radio commentator.

"I am conscious that I am not a typical man," Russian wrestling legend Alexander Karelin told Sports Illustrated in 1991. Karelin is considered the greatest Greco-Roman wrestler of all time, with three Olympic gold medals, nine world championships and 12 European championships.

Shaped by his childhood in Siberia, Karelin became extreme in his approach to wrestling. "I train every day of my life as they have never trained a day in theirs," he said. He once carried a refrigerator up eight flights of stairs.

Ty Cobb, who led the American League in batting 11 times, carried an extreme attitude his entire life. Not long before he died, Cobb attended an Old Timers Day. A reporter approached him and asked, "Ty, what do you suppose you'd hit if you were playing today?" The reporter was surprised when Cobb answered, "About .300."

"Only .300?" the reporter said. "You had the highest batting average of all time. You would hit only .300 today?"

"Well," replied Cobb, "you have to remember that now I'm 67 years old."

Cobb backed up his attitude with extreme action. In his book "My Life in Baseball: The True Record," he described how he got out of a slump. Knowing that success with the bat involved hitting the ball to the middle of the field, Cobb worked on that relentlessly.

He placed a towel in the middle of the field and bunted balls so that they landed directly on the towel. He then moved the towel farther and farther away from home plate, all the while trying to hit the ball directly to it. It took hours.

Has anyone else ever practiced like that? Not to my knowledge. But few people have ever been as driven as Cobb. "I've got to be first all the time — in everything."

"I had to fight all my life to survive," he said. "They were all against me... but I beat them and left them in the ditch."

You find extreme characters in all fields.

"I'm crazy, and I don't pretend to be anything else," designer Calvin Klein once said. Added wrestler Dan Gable, "I know I am extreme."

English composer Michael Tippett made this observation about Beethoven: "He suppressed everything, his personal life disappeared until he was locked inside. That is a figure quite extreme."

Nikola Tesla, pioneer in electricity, liked to weigh and measure his food before he ate it. He would not stay in any hotel room unless the number was divisible by three. He had an extreme hunger for measurement, observation and experimentation.

"I do not think there is any thrill that can go through the human heart like that felt by the inventor as he sees some creation of the brain unfolding to success," Tesla said. "Such emotions make a man forget food, sleep, friends, love, everything."

Comedian W.C. Fields made a crucial decision early in life. He vowed that he would never try to compromise, blend in or be anything but himself. The result? His distinctive voice, delivery, mannerisms and quotes all became part of our culture, and remain so today.

"A comic should suffer as much over a single line as a man with a hernia would in picking up a heavy barbell," Fields once said.

Fred Shero, who coached the Philadelphia Flyers to two straight Stanley Cup championships, tried several extreme techniques with his team. For instance, he copied certain elements of the style played by the Soviet Union. That in itself was extreme in the 1970s, when the Cold War between the United States and the Soviets was still raging. Back then, anything from Russia was something to be feared, not to be admired and certainly not to be copied. But Shero liked the way the Soviets moved.

Shero sometimes used tennis balls instead of pucks in his practices, explaining that his players would find it much easier to handle a puck after trying to control a bouncing ball. At least once, he ran a drill incorrectly, just to see if the players were paying attention. One of them, team captain Bobby Clarke, was, and he confronted Shero over it. That in itself was extreme!

Baseball Hall of Famer Rogers Hornsby refused to watch movies or even read, for fear it would hurt his eyesight. When asked what he did in the winter, Hornsby replied, "I stare out the window and wait for spring."

Annika Sorenstam embarked on a grueling training regimen after becoming the world's best female golfer. Not before. After. She expanded her comfort zone by playing in events with men. "I've learned a lot about my game every time I play golf in a men's event," she said.

Whether in wrestling, golf or any other endeavor, world-class performers take their interests to an extreme. "The kind of commitment I find among the best performers across virtually every field is a single-minded passion for what they do," said Jim Collins, author of "Good to Great."

These performers express their passion with at least three qualities that separate them from others: They set extraordinary goals, they train with these goals in mind; and they can deal with discomfort.

Setting Extraordinary Goals

Baseball slugger Ted Williams had a goal that was as simple as it was grand. He said: "A man has to have goals -- for a day, for a lifetime -- and that was mine, to have people say, 'There goes Ted Williams, the greatest hitter who ever lived.'"

Williams did more than dream about being great. He made hitting a baseball his life's work. He thought about it constantly. He could talk about it by the hour.

It's no surprise that by at least one definition -- on-base percentage -- Williams achieved his goal of being the best. He reached base 48.2 percent of the times he batted. Through all of baseball history, no regular ever did better.

In the early 1960s, President John F. Kennedy gave the world a clear example of extreme goal-setting with his vision for the U.S. space program.

"I believe that this nation should commit itself to achieving the goal, before this decade is out, of landing a man on the moon and returning him safely to the Earth," Kennedy said. Elaborating on that goal in another speech, Kennedy said, "We choose to go to the moon in this decade and do the other things, not because they are easy, but because they are hard, because that goal will serve to organize and measure the best of our energies and skills."

Kennedy knew, and you will find out, that setting great goals will awaken strengths and abilities you never knew you had. Great goals will make you stronger, smarter, tougher, more resourceful.

Kennedy never lived to see man set foot on the moon, but his goal helped point a whole nation to the task. Today we use inventions from the space program, including scratch-resistant lenses, ear thermometers, shoe insoles and, of course, long-distance communications.

"Make no little plans, said Daniel Burnham, a famed American architect. "They have no magic to stir men's blood. ... Make big plans; aim high in hope and work."

Football coach Bill Parcells agrees. "If you don't dream big dreams for yourself," he said, "who will?"

Staying Connected

People come from all over the world to watch the women's volleyball team practice at the University of Washington. Coach Jim McLaughlin preaches the mental game to go along with the physical. He speaks about being connected in practice. For McLaughlin, just doing what the coach says is not enough. He wants his players to remember why they're doing the drill. He wants them to form a connection between what they're doing now and what it might mean the next time they play.

John Vill'Neuve preached the same message in his lab in Bergen County, New Jersey. He never wanted preparation on the spaceship to become sterile, impersonal, theoretical. He reminded his workers about the flesh and blood that would be aboard. "When these men are in space, they can't stop for repairs," he would lecture his team. "It has to be done right."

Connected practice is the highest level of practice. It gives focus and purpose to even the smallest details. Imagine learning to pack a parachute if you knew that you would be using it in a week. There would be no small details!

Dealing With Discomfort

Greta Waitz, great marathon champion, once told an interviewer all you need to know about practicing for success.

"I prefer to train in the dark, cold winter months when it takes a stern attitude to get out of bed before dawn and head out the door to below-freezing weather conditions," she said. "Anyone can run on a nice, warm, brisk day."

Great performers have left ease behind. They live in an uncomfortable world. They practice outside the area of their competence. As soon as they master something, they move on to something else.

Imagine living in this world. It's like being at a never-ending dinner party where you don't know anyone. Or trying to get by in a foreign country where you don't speak the language.

Tom Coughlin, who led the Giants to Super Bowl crowns in 2008 and 2012, once said, "I never want them too comfortable. ... That's not what this is about."

Those who are willing to be uncomfortable can win great rewards, both in the long and short term. For instance, how would you like to make thousands and thousands of dollars for just a few weeks of work? You can do it. Just go to Alaska and get a job as a crab fisherman. You'll be cold, wet, tired and hungry most of the time. You won't even have time for a bathroom break, so you'll have to stay near the rail. You'll never have the luxury of putting off a task until the conditions improve. You'll have to perform in weather that would keep most people curled up by the fire. If you can survive all this, you can make lots of money.

My favorite quote is, "Some people think the battle is against others. The winner understands that the struggle is within the self."

Everyone has weaknesses. Winners work on theirs. Whether it's laziness, lack of organization, inconsistency, poor diet or timidity, winners identify what needs to be corrected and then make it happen.

Here's a trick question. Who was the first person to conquer Mount Everest? Answer: No one. Mount Everest is still there; no one has conquered it. Many people have climbed it by conquering something in themselves, like fear, lack of physical strength, poor planning skills, etc.

So the formula for world-class improvement is the same as for crabbing in Alaska or climbing Mount Everest. There are great rewards if you are willing to do things that other people are not willing to do. If you can become comfortable with being uncomfortable, you can climb Everest, win a marathon, qualify for the Olympics, go to the Hall of Fame or, best of all, get much better at what you do.

CHAPTER TWELVE

Make It Your Story

"The first requisite of success is the ability to apply your physical and mental energies to one problem without growing weary." -- **THOMAS EDISON**

An old sports writer friend once told a story about Moe Berg, a one-of-a-kind ballplayer who read 10 newspapers a day and happened to be an atomic spy for the United States.

Berg was a mediocre batter, but he did speak seven languages, prompting Dave Harris, an outfielder for the Washington Senators, to say, "Yeah, I know, and he can't hit in any of them."

Anyway, as the story goes, Berg's intellect and skill in languages won him an invitation to teach baseball in Japan in the early 1930s. At first Berg protested, saying that he didn't speak the language. He made the trip anyway, and when it was time to go home, someone noticed Berg speaking to a dignitary in Japanese.

"I thought you didn't speak Japanese," the person said.

"Yes," replied Berg, "but that was a month ago."

It turns out that when you look at the details of Berg's life, the story is really more legend than history. But there are enough bits of truth in there to convey Berg's passion for languages. He craved learning, and was fascinated even by accents. He loved it all.

On the other hand, the story of Jeremy Lin is, without a doubt, true. He came to the American -- and international -- stage in early 2012 and created what newspapers called "Linsanity."

He helped the New York Knicks to a series of improbable victories, and the more people looked into his background, the more fascinated they became. Lin was barely recruited out of high school, was unappreciated upon graduation, and was cut by two NBA teams. Despite all that lack of recognition and respect, Lin made it big in New York. He became such a hit on Broadway that he was soon invited to the NBA's All-Star weekend.

More than anything, Lin spawned a wave of soul-searching among sports teams and anyone else who is in the business of finding and acquiring talent. How, they had to ask themselves, could so many people have been so wrong about Jeremy Lin? What did they miss about him? And who else are they overlooking?

If it's any consolation to these people, maybe there's more to Lin's story than simply getting overlooked. Maybe he just kept getting better and better, while other players leveled off.

Lin got where he did the same way that Berg did: endless fascination. Lin kept his passion for basketball even after being passed up by so-called experts. Just as Berg loved to read, study and learn new things, Lin spent lonely hours in the gym, working on his game.

"When you're following your energy and doing what you want all the time, the distinction between work and play dissolves," said Shakti Gawain, author and pioneer in the field of personal development.

To Lin and Berg, what we call work is actually a form of play. They stay fascinated long after most other people lose interest. In doing so, they are actually fighting nature. Call it The Novelty Paradox. Here's how it works:

As humans, we are programmed to keep fascination under control. We have to, or else we would never move on to new things and to other problems. Babies are drawn to shapes, colors, numbers, textures and sounds. If they ever got stuck on just one of those, they would never go to the others. To guard against stagnation, something in the brain takes over and says, for example, "OK, that's the color blue. I get it. Let's move on." Things that were new soon become commonplace.

All of life is a tug-of-war between the familiar and the fresh. I experience it often on my trips into New York City. I walk through Times Square, where you can see the tourists gazing at the sights with wonder in their eyes. To them, it's all new. Some have spent years saving for this once-in-a-lifetime trip.

For me, it's not new, even though I make a conscious effort to see Times Square through a tourist's eyes, to keep it fresh and never lose the sense of wonder. It's not easy. Distractions get in the way. Some nights I want to get home quickly, so I rush through this landmark without even noticing. Sometimes I get impatient with the crowds blocking the street.

It's the same way with most people. They see things with wonder at the start, then the novelty wears off. Distractions get in the way. In the tug-of-war, the familiar wins.

World-class performers are different. They manage to keep this sense of newness. Author Jack Kerouac spoke with admiration of this kind of person. "The only people for me are the mad ones, the ones who are mad to live ... the ones who never yawn or say a commonplace thing, but burn, burn, burn," he said.

If you decide to burn, burn, burn, your story can match any of the ones cited in this book. And that's the point. We've talked of John Vill'Neuve, Tom Fleming, Ralph Lauren, Ty Cobb, Mr. Amateau. They all have great stories. Now it's time to write your story. It's time for you to show yourself, and others, what you can do when you eat your daily orange with focus and care.

When it comes to approaching each day with focus and care, few people can match those recovering from addiction. They have suffered so much through their disease that they want desperately to become sober. They are willing to try anything. They have found what a friend of mine calls the gift of desperation. If you can practice with this kind of desperation, with a sense that you want to get everything you can out of your work, you can improve dramatically.

I wish you that gift of desperation in your practice hours. I hope that you burn, burn burn.

Thank you for reading this book. I hope it makes all the difference in your life. It's something I have been wanting to finish for a long time, and it's a joyous and humbling feeling to have done so. I give thanks.